FOR DOG'S SAKE!

FOR DOG'S SAKE!

A simple guide to protecting your pup from
unsafe foods, everyday dangers,
and bad situations

AMY LUWIS

**Andrews McMeel
Publishing®**
a division of Andrews McMeel Universal

Other books by Amy Luwis

Yoga to the Rescue: Remedies for Real Girls

Yoga to the Rescue: Ageless Beauty

DISCLAIMER

It's always
about the dogs . . .

This book is intended for
educational purposes only. It is
not intended to be a substitute
for professional veterinarian
advice, diagnosis, or treatment.
Always seek the advice of your
veterinarian with any questions
you may have regarding your
dog. If you think your dog has
a medical emergency, call
or visit your veterinarian or
local veterinary emergency
hospital immediately.

DR. DOG

For the millions of dogs in shelters waiting for a home.

And for my parents, who taught me how
to be kind to all living things.

CONTENTS

DANGERS IN THE GREAT OUTDOORS AND BEYOND • 42

FOODS TOXIC TO DOGS • 59

Please read on. I promise you'll learn a lot and have fun while doing it.

MOSTLY NONTOXIC, BUT RISKY . . . PROCEED WITH CAUTION • 80

FOREWORD

In my thirty-six years practicing veterinary medicine, I've seen almost every accident, poisoning, injury, and trauma that can happen to a dog. The world we live in is a very dangerous one for dogs, but it's inherent in us to provide them with a safe environment. Every aspect of our canine companions' safety and quality of life depends on us and the nurturing environment we provide. Unfortunately, we often overlook things in our homes and yards that are potential hazards due to the curious natures and strong survival instincts of our canine friends.

This great little book is as much useful to new dog owners as it is to those with years of experience. Amy's clear and precise instruction, based on her extensive research and experience of the everyday hazards dogs face, makes this a fantastic reference book for the home. The topics she covers, ranging from accident prevention and first-aid treatment to poisonous plant identification and common food toxicities, represent just a few of the valuable lessons every dog owner should know and can now reference quickly. Before reading this book, would you know how to perform the doggy Heimlich maneuver in that off-chance a dog biscuit slipped down the wrong pipe?

My favorite thing about this book is Amy's artwork. Not only are her clever illustrations helpful visual references to her instructions, they also lend a welcome breath of fresh air and humor that will keep you coming back for another look.

Charles Loops, DVM

Veterinarian for thirty-six years specializing in homeopathic medicine

INTRODUCTION

Every hour of every day, dogs get hurt. What's worse, many are harmed in their very own homes by well-meaning, but woefully uninformed humans. Yes, you, who love them more than baby seals and cupcakes, are unknowingly putting them in harm's way.

Some of the most dangerous things for your dog are common foods and medications lurking in dog-enticing locations. Did you know that just three ounces of baker's chocolate can kill a fifteen-pound dog? Or that human medications are the number-one cause of pet poisoning? Or that innocent snow globes are loaded with lethal antifreeze? If you are not aware of these dangers and have thoughts of using this book to level a table or use it as a handy drink coaster, please consider reading it instead.

My mission in creating this book is to help dog parents, dog lovers, dog sitters, and anyone who cares about our canine friends, gain knowledge and awareness about dog dangers, so they can protect their pups and hopefully prevent disasters.

I've purposefully kept this book streamlined and fun, so you won't get overwhelmed with too much information or fall asleep while perusing its important pages.

I hope you enjoy learning a few things that just might save your dog's life.

Amy Luwis

DOGGY 101: SOME BASICS

Physical Signs of a Healthy Dog

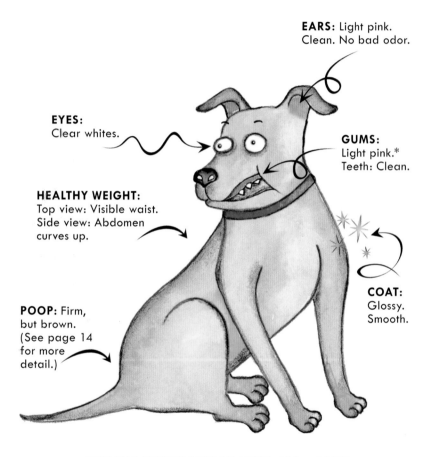

EARS: Light pink. Clean. No bad odor.

EYES: Clear whites.

GUMS: Light pink.* Teeth: Clean.

HEALTHY WEIGHT: Top view: Visible waist. Side view: Abdomen curves up.

COAT: Glossy. Smooth.

POOP: Firm, but brown. (See page 14 for more detail.)

NORMAL TEMPERATURE RANGE: 100 to 102°F

*If your dog has naturally dark gums, then you can check the color of the inside of eyelids by pulling gently down on the lower lid, which should be light pink.

8 Things That Will Keep Your Dog Healthier

1. Good Grooming

Good grooming is not just about a cute haircut. It's about overall well-being.

FUR: Brush your dog several times a week, even if he has short hair.

EARS: Check ears once a week. They should be free of debris and redness, and smell good, not stinky.

NAILS: Trim dog nails a sliver at a time to avoid cutting into the quick (the part of the nail that contains blood vessels). Nails that grow too long can grow into paw pads and skin, causing pain and infection.

2. Socialization and Exercise

Socialization and exercise are very important to the overall well-being and happiness of your dog. They provide mental stimulation, reduce stress, and provide the opportunity to develop skills for coping with new experiences in a positive way.

3. A Safe, Comfortable Environment

Whether or not your dog sleeps in your bed, he needs his very own "safe spot" to retreat to, such as a crate and/or comfortable bed. The ideal dog bed should be comfortable and cater to your dog's needs. An older dog may need orthopedic support and a fearful dog may need a walled dog bed. All beds should be easily washable.

4. A Healthy Diet

I know you like the pretty colors in my kibble, but I refuse to eat artificial coloring.

Give your dog a nutritionally balanced diet and access to clean, fresh water. Avoid food with artificial ingredients, by-products, and fillers. MSG is hidden in many foods under false names, such as "hydrolyzed protein" (visit: www.truthinlabeling.org/hiddensources for more information).

Keep informed about pet food and treat recalls: www.fda.gov/AnimalVeterinary/SafetyHealth/RecallsWithdrawals

The Skinny on Bowls

Food and water bowls are used all day, every day by your dog, so be sure to purchase safe, durable options:

☠ Plastic and painted ceramic bowls can leach chemicals into your dog's food and water.

☠ Studies have shown high levels of lead in some ceramic dog bowls. So look for bowls that have lead-free, food-grade glazes.

☠ Plastic is easily scratched and chewed, leaving crevices for harmful bacteria to build up.

Stainless steel is a safe choice, but be careful about the origin and quality of the bowls you choose. There are documented cases of stainless-steel dog bowls from India testing positive for high levels of lead, and bowls from China that were found to be radioactive.

Sturdy glass is a safe choice. It doesn't attract bacteria. It cleans easily and is dishwasher safe.

WHO KNEW? Plastic Dish Nasal Dermatitis: This is a localized form of depigmentation that affects the nose and lips. It is caused by eating out of plastic and rubber dishes that contain the chemical p-benzyl hydroquinone. This chemical is absorbed through the skin and inhibits the synthesis of melanin. —WebMD.com

5. Regular Veterinary Appointments

Routine visits to your vet can help catch health problems before they become severe and difficult to treat.

My vet told me that I need to lose weight, but I think I'm just retaining water.

6. Proper Dental Care

Dental disease can lead to serious problems with your dog's organs, such as the heart, liver, and kidneys, so caring for your dog's teeth and gums is very important.

Brush your dog's teeth daily.

Dental disease is the most common disease seen by veterinarians: 70 to 85 percent of pets over two years old have some form of dental disease.

☠ Never use human toothpaste to clean your dog's teeth (xylitol is deadly to dogs and many human toothpastes contain this sweetener).

7. Compassion

Many dogs are turned in to shelters because of behavior problems that could have been easily resolved, so do your best to remedy problems on your own or with the assistance of a compassionate trainer.

Keep in mind that behavior problems are not always an isolated issue. For instance, a dog who has an abrupt personality change may have developed an underlying health issue. Health issues that can affect your dog's behavior include: arthritis, thyroid problems, infections, sore teeth, digestive issues, allergies, hearing and eyesight loss, cancer, and others.

8. Spaying or Neutering Your Dog*

Dogs who have this surgery tend to live longer, be healthier, and have fewer behavioral issues.

By spaying/neutering your dog, you are also a positive force in helping reduce the severe problem of pet overpopulation.

I just made boom-boom with the neighbor's hottie Chihuahua.

SPAY NEUTER

I would just like a cuddle and a warm lap.

* If you cannot afford to spay/neuter your dog, there are organizations that will help. Check the "Resources" section of this book for assistance.

Physical Signs of a Not-So-Healthy Dog

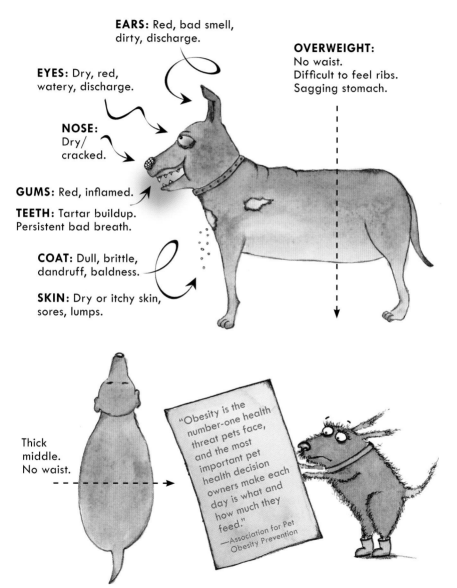

EARS: Red, bad smell, dirty, discharge.

EYES: Dry, red, watery, discharge.

NOSE: Dry/ cracked.

OVERWEIGHT: No waist. Difficult to feel ribs. Sagging stomach.

GUMS: Red, inflamed.

TEETH: Tartar buildup. Persistent bad breath.

COAT: Dull, brittle, dandruff, baldness.

SKIN: Dry or itchy skin, sores, lumps.

Thick middle. No waist.

"Obesity is the number-one health threat pets face, and the most important pet health decision owners make each day is what and how much they feed."
—Association for Pet Obesity Prevention

Common Symptoms of Poisoning and Illness

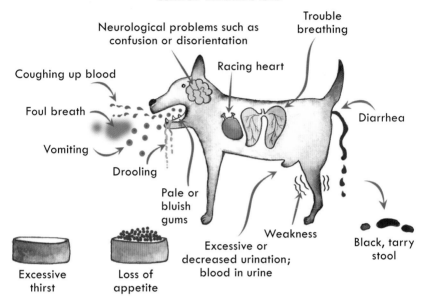

Neurological problems such as confusion or disorientation

Trouble breathing

Coughing up blood

Racing heart

Foul breath

Diarrhea

Vomiting

Drooling

Pale or bluish gums

Weakness

Excessive or decreased urination; blood in urine

Black, tarry stool

Excessive thirst

Loss of appetite

Symptoms can show up immediately or they can develop over time, so it's always smart to pay attention to any changes in your dog's behavior and health.

If you suspect that your dog has been poisoned, in most cases the sooner you get treatment, the better the outcome. If you can, take the substance/packaging with you to the vet, so he or she can see what your pet ingested and take appropriate action.

HELPFUL HINT Always keep these phone numbers handy and visible for the entire family and for anyone taking care of your dog(s): • 24-hour emergency vet
• Your regular vet
• Pet poison helpline

It is also a good idea to keep medical records and medications handy and visible.

Keep the Following in Mind

Like humans, all dogs are different. There is no "one size fits all" when it comes to reactions to toxic substances and illness. The following factors all play a role:

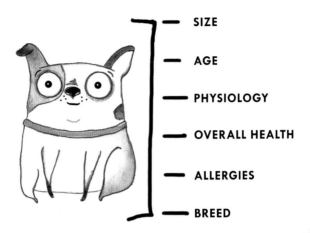

- **SIZE**
- **AGE**
- **PHYSIOLOGY**
- **OVERALL HEALTH**
- **ALLERGIES**
- **BREED**

The amount of the toxic substance ingested, absorbed, or inhaled and what part is ingested (leaves, fruit, pit, etc.) also play a role.

Eating and drinking are not the only ways your dog can be poisoned. They can also . . .

roll in or walk on pesticides and absorb them through their skin, as well as lick them off.

inhale/breathe in toxic substances such as pesticides and paint.

The Scoop on Poop

Take your pup's poop seriously because it reveals a wealth of information about overall health.

THE PERFECT POOP

Chocolate-brown. Firm, but moist. Segmented log shape. Consistency of Play-Doh. Light odor.

BLACK/TARRY

May indicate a large amount of blood in the stool.

BRIGHT RED STREAKS

Could mean blood in the stool.

GRAY/MUCUS COATING

Can indicate inadequate digestion and malabsorption of nutrients.

YELLOW/ORANGE

Can indicate problems with the liver, gallbladder, or pancreas.

COW PATTY/SOFT-SERVE

Can be due to a change in diet or may be a sign of illness or infection.

LIQUID/DIARRHEA

If persistent, can indicate a viral or intestinal infection. (Caution: Dogs with diarrhea are at high risk of dehydration.)

DRY CHUNKS

May indicate dehydration or kidney disease.

WHITE RICE

Rice-shaped flecks or spaghetti-like strands may be worms.

CLUMPS OF HAIR

Can be due to allergies or other medical conditions.

UNDIGESTED FOOD

Can indicate food intolerance or allergy.

FOREIGN OBJECTS

Need to keep things out of reach. Can cause obstruction.

WARNING: Abnormal poop patterns are a red flag that something is wrong. Noticing changes early could prevent a problem and even save your dog's life, so learn to be a poop sleuth!

PUMPKIN MAGIC!

Pumpkin works miracles in everyday cases of diarrhea or constipation. Pumpkin is a "normalizer" —it softens hard stools and will firm up a loose stool. Serve fresh-cooked pumpkin or canned pumpkin puree.

COMMON HOUSEHOLD DANGERS

PRESCRIPTION DRUGS TO PENNIES

Homes are brimming with enticing smells, shiny objects, and curiosities. Dogs explore their world by: sniffing, chewing, licking, and eating, so . . . everything is a potential snack or toy!

Common accidents such as poisoning, choking, intestinal obstruction, drowning, falls, and electric cord shock can be avoided with awareness and prevention.

Prescription Drugs and Over-the-Counter Medicines

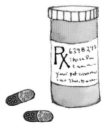 

Pain killers (including aspirin, acetaminophen, and ibuprofen), cold medicines, anticancer drugs, antidepressants, vitamins, and diet pills can be deadly.

Keep medicine and vitamin containers away from dogs. Be vigilant about finding and discarding dropped pills. Make sure handbags and suitcases with pills are safely out of reach.

Rodenticides

Dogs often fall victim to these lethal products because they are made to be enticing. Dogs can also be greatly harmed by eating rats or mice who have ingested rodenticides.

Rodenticide poisoning is one of the most commonly reported poisonings according to the veterinarians at Pet Poison Helpline.

Insecticide Bait

The most common insecticides that dogs get into are ant and roach baits. Like rodenticides, they often have enticing flavors such as peanut butter.

"Pets, like children, have a small body size and are exceedingly vulnerable to pesticides."
—Jay Feldman, founder of Beyond Pesticides

Household Cleaners

Especially concentrated ones are highly toxic for dogs. Consider using natural, organic cleaning solutions instead.

Matches

Matches contain hazardous chemicals, including potassium nitrate, which is dangerous to dogs. Matches can also contain charcoal or sulfur and coloring agents, which are potentially dangerous heavy metals.

Batteries

Batteries can be very dangerous if ingested. Alkaline or acidic material can leak out, resulting in severe corrosive damage.

Tobacco

The effects nicotine has on a dog are far worse than on humans. Cigarettes, cigars, butts, nicotine patches, nicotine gum, and chewing tobacco contain nicotine, which can cause illness and even death.

Flea and Tick Control Products

These products can cause serious toxic reactions when used incorrectly. This includes topical, shampoos, sprays, dips, and household treatments.

Pennies

Pennies minted after 1982 contain a high level of zinc, which can cause kidney failure if swallowed.

WHO KNEW? According to the ASPCA Animal Poison Control Center, zinc poisoning in dogs can occur with the ingestion of a single penny.

MDI Glue

An especially harmful substance called methylene diphenyl diisocyanate (MDI) is often found in wood, construction, and high-strength glues.

Dogs love the smell and taste of many MDI-based glues.

CHOMP!
CHOMP!

A tiny amount of glue expands into a huge amount . . . quickly.

This can be very serious, even fatal, so keep MDI-based glues out of reach.

Because these glues are a common household item and because they smell and taste great to dogs, MDI-glue inges-tion is a common emergency seen by many vets, and is very serious. If swallowed, any amount of this glue can expand to a size that may cause an intestinal blockage where emergency surgery could be necessary.

Trash

Bacteria, mold, spoiled food, dental floss, sharp objects, plastic wrap, empty snack bags, discarded medication, bones, and more are all lurking in the trash, and can cause everything from mild stomach upset to choking to suffocating to food poisoning.

 TIP Use trash cans with lids that dogs can't open, or keep the can in a closed cupboard or up high so your dog can't reach it. If your dog has learned to open cupboard doors, install childproof latches.

Common Choking Hazards

Most dogs will chew and swallow almost anything. Some objects may pass through easily, but others could get stuck in the throat or intestines.

One of the top reasons dogs go to the vet is because they've ingested something they shouldn't have.

Buttons

Buttons come in all different shapes, sizes, and materials, and are enticing to a curious dog.

Dental Floss

Dental floss is appealing (especially used floss), easy to swallow, and can cause serious intestinal blockages and strangulation.

Balls

Balls that are too small can get lodged in the throat, and any ball that is chewable can become a choking hazard.

Coins

Not only are coins a choking hazard, but pennies minted after 1982 contain a high level of zinc which can cause kidney failure if swallowed.

Rubber Bands

With the popularity of bracelet-making using rubber bands, more and more vets are seeing dogs that have ingested rubber bands. Along with being a choking hazard, rubber bands can get stuck in the intestine, which can lead to a rupture of the intestines.

Pins

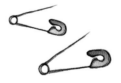

Not only are safety pins and straight pins a choking hazard, they can also cause internal punctures.

Hard Candy and Candy Wrappers

These small treats can easily be inhaled into the windpipe and cause choking.

Yarn, String, and Thread

String, yarn, and thread are easy to swallow and can cause intestinal blockages and strangulation.

Plastic Bags and Plastic Wrap

Plastic wrap is a major choking hazard for dogs. It is appealing because it often has remnants of food on it.

Toys (Human and Dog)

Avoid flimsy toys and toys with lots of little parts that can be chewed off. Many toys have plastic squeaky bubbles inside that are the perfect choking hazard. To be safe, always supervise your dog when playing with toys.

Socks

Dirty socks and undergarments are enticing to many dogs. In addition to potentially causing difficult bowel movements, they can cause serious intestinal blockages.

Deadly Handbags

GUMS AND MINTS WITH XYLITOL Most sugarless gums and some candy and mints contain xylitol, a sweetener that can be fatal to dogs.

MEDICATIONS/PILLS Prescription medications and over-the-counter products, including NSAIDs (e.g., Advil, Aleve, and Motrin), supplements, and cough and cold relievers, can all be danerous or even fatal to dogs.

NICOTINE PRODUCTS Cigarettes, chewing tobacco, and nicotine gum are all toxic to dogs. Depending on their strength, ingesting as few as three cigarettes can be fatal for smaller dogs.

HAND SANITIZER AND PERFUME These contain high amounts of alcohol (ethanol), which is toxic to dogs.

I think the red really brings out your eyes.

HELPFUL HINT Keep purses out of reach of curious noses—in a cupboard, a drawer, or on a high shelf.

Prevention

Keep dangers safely out of reach before your dog licks them, makes a meal of them, rolls in them, or chokes on them.

Reduce the risks even further by not bringing dangers into your home in the first place, and when necessary, consider using safer alternatives, such as natural and organic cleaners.

Keep very, very far away.

TOO CLOSE.

Yummy!

Do not work with toxic substances in the same room as your dog.

Do not leave a mess.
Clean up spills.

Ring!
Ring!

Do not leave toxic
substances out
unattended.

tap
tap
taaap
TAP

HELPFUL HINT Read labels
carefully and familiarize yourself
with dangerous ingredients.

Household Plants

More than seven hundred household plants contain toxic substances that may harm your dog if ingested. Reactions to toxicity range from mild to life threatening.

Toxic Houseplants

Aloe Vera

Asparagus Fern

Dracaena

Dumb Cane

Elephant Ear (Alocasia)

Jade

Peace Lily

Philodendron

Sago Palm

Satin Pathos

Some Safe Houseplants

Achira

African Daisy

African Violet

Aluminum Plant

American Rubber Plant

Bamboo Palm

Begonia

Ferns (Maidenhair,
Boston, and Bird's Nest)

Orchids

Peperomia

Prayer Plant

Purple Waffle Plant

Spider Plant

Zebra Haworthia

Bonus!
Puppy Safety Tips!

ELECTRICAL Invest in cord protectors and outlet covers. Tape cords to walls, unplug them, and spray with a bitter pet spray.

DANGLING OBJECTS Keep window blind cords, potted plants, etc., out of reach.

TABLES Tablecloths can be pulled off tables along with heavy objects.

WATER Fence off pools and garden ponds to prevent access. Don't leave a bucket of water out—a puppy can drown in it.

INSTALL CHILD-PROOFING Locking latches for low cabinets, covers for electrical outlets, and baby gates are good options.

RECLINERS Puppies can easily get trapped in reclining chairs, so keep them closed when not in use.

TOYS Avoid those that can be ripped apart easily and contain small removable parts.

BE TIDY Check under beds and sofas for enticing objects, from rubber bands to paperclips to socks and undies. Be diligent about keeping choking hazards off the floor.

THE BACKYARD, GARAGE, AND SHED
ANTIFREEZE TO RODENTICIDES

An extravaganza of dangerous goodies lurk in forgotten corners of garages and sheds, and yards are bursting with toxins for curious dogs.

According to the American Society for the Prevention of Cruelty to Animals Animal Control Center, experts field thousands of calls about pets that have had potentially hazardous contact with insecticides, weed killer, and pet-toxic plants.

TASTY-YUM-YUM
RODENT KILLER
GUARANTEED to torture every fuzzy critter in your home or your money back!

Antifreeze

Antifreezes that contain ethylene glycol are deadly to dogs. They have an enticing, sweet taste and can leak from vehicles onto the ground and into puddles.

Fertilizer

While some fertilizers can be safe to dogs, others that contain iron, insecticides, and blood and bone meal (also mentioned in this section) can be very unsafe.

Blood Meal and Bone Meal

Blood meal ingestion can lead to severe pancreatitis and also lead to a cement-like blockage in the gastrointestinal system.

Blood meal containing iron can lead to iron toxicity.

Plant Bulbs

Tulips, hyacinths, daffodils, and narcissus can be particularly dangerous to dogs, especially the bulbs.

Cocoa Mulch

Made from the discarded shells of cocoa beans, this chocolate-like mulch is attractive to dogs. Cocoa mulch contains theobromine and caffeine, both toxic to dogs.

Compost

Good for the environment and your garden, bad for your dog. As organic matter decomposes, toxic molds can grow, so keep your compost covered/fenced off.

Insecticide/Pesticide

Most insecticides and pesticides are basic irritants to dogs with unknown long-term effects. And some contain organophosphates that can be life threatening when consumed in a high enough dose.

Research on phenoxy herbicides shows that they increase the incidence of cancer.

Fencing

Especially for escape artists and wanderers, make sure you:

- Secure holes and gaps
- Repair broken fencing
- Eliminate sharp fence parts

Make sure your dog can't:

- Squeeze through
- Leap over
- Dig under
- Unlatch a gate

Blue-Green Algae (Cyanobacteria)

These are tiny bacteria found in ponds, lakes, streams, and brackish water. Some—not all—blue-green algae produces toxins that are dangerous to dogs. Dogs who swim in and drink contaminated water could be fatally poisoned.

Blue-green algae flourishes in ponds where there is little air circulation, during droughts, and in hot weather, so be extra vigilant with your dog under these conditions.

Blue-green algae can form a thick layer on the water's surface.

Fly Bait

The toxic chemical methomyl is an active ingredient in fly baits and other insecticides. It is harmful when ingested, inhaled, or absorbed through the skin.

Snail and Slug Bait

Snail/slug bait contains metaldehyde, which is lethal to dogs. Pellets are often combined with enticing things such as molasses. It is in your dog's best interest to not use these baits in your yard.

Pool Supplies

Undiluted pool chemicals can be life threatening, so keep pool chemicals in a secure area and never leave open containers laying around.

Rodenticides

Dogs often fall victim to these lethal products because they are made to be enticing. Dogs can also be greatly harmed by eating rats, mice, and birds that have ingested rodenticides.

Rock Salt and Salt-Based Ice-Melting Products

Ice-melting products cover roads, driveways, sidewalks, and any place snow is required to melt, and it is very bad for dogs, both internally and externally. Dogs walk in it, roll in it, drag in it, and lick it off their paws ingesting poisonous chemicals.

Salt can heat up to 175°F, not only burning skin and paws, but when ingested, internal burns of the mouth and digestive tract, as well.

Gets frozen and stuck between paws.

Can cause dermatitis, inflammation of the paws, and serious gastrointestinal problems.

CAUTION
Ice-melting products are <u>not</u> ordinary table salt; they contain potent chemicals, such as sodium chloride, that are very harmful to dogs.

Consider acquiring a set of dog booties to protect paws and keep snow from building up between paw pads, which can be very painful.

Reduce the Risk of Exposure

Trim the fur between toe pads.

Wash paws in warm soapy water once inside.

If your dog rolls in contaminated snow, wash him thoroughly.

Trim any fur that may drag through the snow.

Prevention

Keep things safely out of reach of curious dogs, from fertilizer to pool-cleaning supplies to sharp objects and swallowable items such as golf balls. And if they are deadly, such as rodenticides and antifreeze, consider safer alternatives or consider not keeping these items on your property.

Your dog absorbs a lot through his paws, so wipe them well if he walks in toxic substances such as pesticides, and if he's rolled in it, give him a bath.

It is a good idea to wipe your dog's paws after a walk, even if you don't think he's walked in anything toxic.

Outdoor Flowers and Plants

Some of the most dangerous threats to your dog are growing right in your very own backyard. This section covers some of the deadliest and most common flowers and plant. Before you dig up your flower bed, keep in mind that of the thousands of plant and flower species, only a small percentage are truly dangerous and poisonous to dogs.

Consider not planting these varieties if you have a particularly curious dog who enjoys exploring through nibbling the yard and garden.

Azalea

Autumn Crocus

Castor Bean

Chrysanthemum (Mums)

I always knew you
wanted me out
of the house . . .

Cyclamen

Daffodil

Foxglove

Jasmine

Kalanchoe

Oleander

Lily of the Valley

Yew

DANGERS IN THE GREAT OUTDOORS AND BEYOND

A dog's enthusiasm for dark holes, smelly things, moving objects, and tasty mysteries should encourage us to be prepared during outdoor adventures. Here are some of the top dangers to watch for when venturing out with your dog.

I thought she said we were going camping?

Foxtails

Foxtails are grasses with seed awns (the foxtail-shaped tip of the grass blade containing seeds). Foxtails have barbed, razor-sharp needles that are extremely dangerous to dogs.

Foxtails easily attach themselves to a romping dog and can burrow deeper with each movement. They can work their way into any part of your dog. Foxtails are barbed and designed to migrate in one direction.

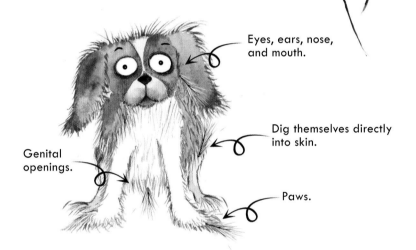

Eyes, ears, nose, and mouth.

Dig themselves directly into skin.

Genital openings.

Paws.

SAFETY TIPS Stay out of areas with foxtails. If your dog has mingled with foxtails, make sure to do a thorough inspection afterward: Brush his coat, feel every inch of the body with hands, and look closely at ears, nose, eyes, underbelly, between toe pads, and underneath the collar.

BE AWARE OF THESE SYMPTOMS Continuous sneezing, pawing at the infected area, violent shaking of head, sores or abscesses, discharge, and coughing.

Mushrooms

The majority of wild-growing mushrooms are not harmful to dogs; however, some contain toxins that are very dangerous to dogs and in some cases can lead to death if ingested. To be safe, it's best to keep your dog away from all wild mushrooms.

"Dogs take a special interest in both *Amanita phalloides* and *Inocybe* species, quite possibly because of their fishy odor. A great many dogs die each year from consuming mushrooms containing amatoxins."

—North American Mycological Association

SOURCES
Wooded areas, marshy grasslands, logs, gardens, and yards. After rainy weather many mushrooms crop up.

 **SAFETY TIPS**

Many dogs have a tendency to eat grass, which can lead to accidentally ingesting mushrooms, so check your yard and garden for mushrooms.

If you suspect that your dog has eaten wild mushrooms, you should contact your vet immediately, even if your dog is not showing any symptoms. If possible, try to get a sample of the mushroom consumed and store in a paper bag or in wax paper, not plastic.

BEWARE
Any wild mushroom should be considered as a potential risk to your dog if ingested, and you should never let your dog eat or sniff around wild mushrooms or fungus of any type.

 WHO KNEW?

Dogs are attracted to certain mushrooms because of how they smell and taste.

The toxicity in mushrooms hits smaller dogs much harder than big dogs.

Perils of Puddles

Just about anything can find its way into a puddle and contaminate it. Anything from deadly bacteria to microscopic protozoa to antifreeze can all be found in puddles.

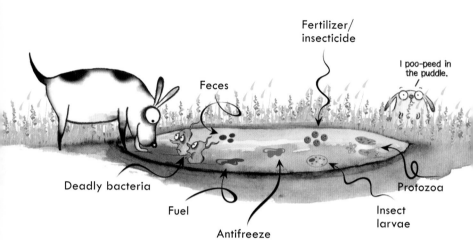

Fertilizer/insecticide

I poo-peed in the puddle.

Feces

Deadly bacteria

Fuel

Antifreeze

Insect larvae

Protozoa

DEADLY BACTERIA Not all dogs become sick when exposed to Leptospirosis, but for those that do, the results can be devastating. Leptospirosis most commonly causes kidney failure.

PROTOZOA GIARDIA These organisms are microscopic protozoa. The most common symptom caused by giardiasis in dogs is diarrhea.

WARNING: Be sure to avoid puddles that have formed in and around parking lots where antifreeze can leak from vehicles. Consumption of only a very tiny amount of antifreeze can kill a dog.

Sticks

Dogs love sticks! But are they worth the risk? Dogs can sustain multiple injuries from sticks ranging from mild trauma to life-threatening damage.

Expert Advice:

"Never throw sticks for dogs. Even if you do it now, never do it again; it is a violent incident that causes real damage."

—Robin Hargreaves, president-elect of the British Veterinary Association

Zoe Halfacree, senior lecturer at the Royal Veterinary College, sees three stick injuries a month—"Owners do not know what the problem is and infections become established before vet attention."

Sticks are often sharp and very dirty. They are loaded with bacteria and fungi, and may contain lungworm.

Pieces of wood being aspirated (inhaled) can lead to possible obstruction, irritation, and/or infection of the respiratory tract. Such wood fragments can also lead to puncture of the trachea or lung tissue, resulting in a chest infection or even damage to the heart, nerves, and/or blood vessels.

Sticks jammed into the ground cause many serious injuries. They can quickly impale the throat, the chest, an eye, and more.

Dogs Who Run with Sticks and Chase Sticks

Sticks can easily pierce the skin, stabbing into eyes, mouths, chest, and neck causing severe injury.

Sticks can splinter in the mouth causing dogs to choke.

Small wood splinters can embed in the tongue, the gums, back of the throat, and under the gum line. Large wood fragments get stuck between teeth and wedged in the roof of the mouth.

WHO KNEW? "Rogue splinters" —pieces of a stick can break off and remain inside, causing problems in the future.

 HANDY TIP Consider alternatives such as Ruff Dawg's "The Stick" and Kong's "Safestix."

Stings and Insect Bites

Bees, wasps, yellow jackets, fire ants, centipedes, spiders, and, of course, fleas can all bite or sting your dog, causing pain and discomfort.

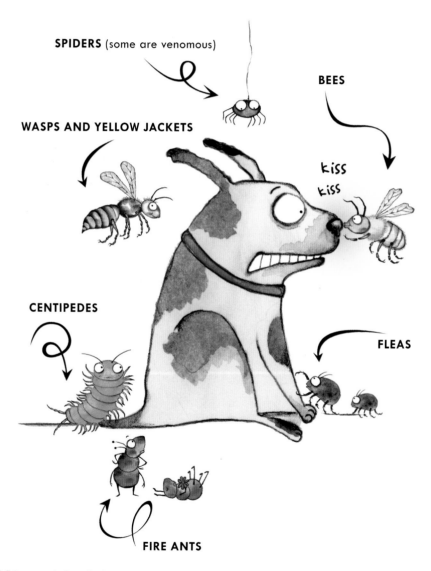

SPIDERS (some are venomous)

BEES

WASPS AND YELLOW JACKETS

kiss kiss

CENTIPEDES

FLEAS

FIRE ANTS

Stings are one of the most common wounds that dogs get, with bee stings topping the list, so watch out for nests in your backyard.

Dogs get stung on their faces most of the time, and a sting on the sensitive nose is particularly painful.

Spider Bites

There are 40,000 known varieties of spiders, but don't panic—many spiders are not even capable of piercing the skin, and only a few are toxic to dogs.

The two spider species in the United States toxic to dogs:

BROWN RECLUSE SPIDER

Known for its violin marking.

WIDOW SPIDER

Known for its red hourglass abdomen marking.

The brown recluse is nocturnal and got its name because of its habits of living hidden under objects in undisturbed areas.

Widow spiders like dark, non-disturbed places such as wood piles, old sheds, and dry wells. A dog may be bitten while indoors or outdoors, as black widows are known to frequent both.

Signs of a Spider Bite

Difficulty breathing if
the bite is on his nose.

It wasn't me,
I swear;
it was my Uncle
Walter.

Swelling at the site
of the bite.

Redness.

Licking/pawing at
the affected area.

Bite marks may be
visible.

Dogs bitten by black widow spiders may show signs of severe muscle pain, cramping, walking as though drunk, tremors, paralysis, drooling, vomiting, and diarrhea.

Dogs bitten by a brown recluse spider may show symptoms such as vomiting, fever, lethargy, and severe skin wounds.

Spider Bite Prevention

Keep in mind that spiders play a crucial role in our ecosystem—without them, insect populations would explode, decimating our food crops, so it's better not to harm spiders that are minding their own business.

I've got a
family back
in Toledo!

Keep dogs out of known spider hangouts: basements, crawl spaces, and outbuildings, such as sheds.

Spot-check and shake out dog towels or blankets before using.

Keep clutter to a minimum. Spiders love nothing better than a dark corner filled with junk.

Cover up and seal openings in your home to avoid uninvited guests.

CAUTION Young and old dogs are at an increased risk for complications due to their weaker immune systems.

Snake Bites

"Snake bites are one of the top ten most common pet injuries."
—Veterinary Pet Insurance Group

Dogs are curious creatures and snakes—with their fascinating smell and slithering bodies—can be irresistible.

WHO KNEW? Most experts agree that a snake can only strike anywhere from half to two-thirds of their body length.

Venomous Snakes in the United States

RATTLESNAKE

COTTONMOUTH/ WATER MOCCASIN

COPPERHEAD

CORAL SNAKE

Many harmless snakes are needlessly killed because they are mistaken for their venomous relatives. The majority of snakes in the United States are not a threat. Consider getting a field guide to help you identify which snakes are harmless and which to avoid.

Some Tips on
How to Prevent Snake Bites

Keep your dog on leash.

Pretty please will you let me off now? There are noooooo snakes here.

Avoid long grasses, bushes, and rocks. Stay on open, clear paths where snakes are more visible.

Experts Recommend:

- Keeping your dog on leash is probably the best safety advice.

- Do not allow your dog to explore holes in the ground, under logs, and areas with nooks and crannies.

- Keep your yard tidy and pathways clear, particularly in the summer months, when rattlesnakes thrive.

- Carefully inspect the area before letting your dog run free in your yard.

- If your dog seems overly curious and enthusiastic about something hidden in the grass, call him away immediately—it could be a snake.

If Your Dog Is Bitten
by a Venomous Snake

1. **STAY CALM.** Try to identify the snake (take a
   photo if you can without getting close).

2. **KEEP YOUR DOG CALM** and as immobile as possible. Movement
   can cause venom to travel more quickly through the bloodstream.

3. **CARRY YOUR DOG** or walk him slowly to your vehicle.

4. **REMOVE HIS COLLAR.** Bites frequently occur on the head
   and can cause severe head and neck swelling.

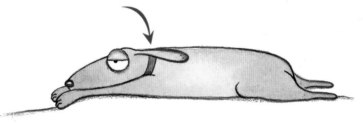

5. **GO DIRECTLY TO A VETERINARIAN** who has antivenom.
   (Call ahead to make sure they have it in stock.)

 TIPS There is a rattlesnake vaccine available.
It won't prevent snake bites, but it hopefully will minimize
the damage.

A venomous snake bite is extremely painful, so use caution when
handling your dog. When you lift him into the car, temporarily muzzle
him or wrap your dog in a blanket. (You can use a strip of t-shirt for a
muzzle if you don't have one.)

Big snakes might strike two or three times before they release venom,
but baby snakes are less cautious and often release all of their venom
at once, making for a very potent bite.

Water Hemlock/Spotted Parsley

This wildflower has been dubbed "the most violently toxic plant that grows in North America" by the USDA. True to its reputation, water hemlock can kill a dog within fifteen minutes of ingestion. It usually grows in wet or damp fields or in swamps.

The most distinguishing feature of the water hemlock is the purple-streaked or spotted stems.

Additional Outdoor Safety Suggestions

☙ Consider a canine life vest if your dog spends time near water. Not all dogs take to water naturally.

☙ Watch out for strong currents, which can whisk a dog away from shore quickly.

☙ Consider investing in a dog-safe sunscreen if your dog spends a lot of time in the sun. Areas with exposed skin and short-haired dogs are more easily burned by the sun.

☙ When hiking and camping, keep an eye out for horseback riders and cyclists and keep your dog on leash or in an orange safety vest during hunting season.

☙ Consider investing in a coat and/or booties for your dog if you hike together often.

☙ Attach a bell to your dog's collar. Hunting bells are loud, so you can hear your dog from far away if he runs off.

FOODS
TOXIC
TO
DOGS

Alcohol

Dogs can die from ingesting alcohol. Alcoholic drinks contain a lot of ethanol, which is toxic to dogs. A dog's kidneys are not meant to process alcohol; even a small amount is damaging.

It's the only way I can relax after a stressful day of marking every blade of grass with my pee, while simultaneously bringing joy and happiness to ALL with my kisses, tail wags, and astonishing cuteness.

SOURCES

Alcoholic beverages; rum-soaked fruitcake; mouthwash; perfume; some medications (such as cough syrup and tinctures); unbaked dough containing yeast; et al.

BEWARE

Ingestion of alcohol can cause dangerous drops in blood sugar, blood pressure, and body temperature. Intoxicated animals can experience seizures and respiratory failure.

SAFETY TIPS

Don't leave alcoholic beverages unattended and don't give your dog alcohol for fun. Clean up alcohol spills before your pup can lick it up.

WHO KNEW?

If your dog eats raw yeast dough, the yeast will ferment in his gastro-intestinal tract—turning into alcohol. Alcohol from the fermenting yeast is rapidly absorbed into the bloodstream, quickly resulting in alcohol poisoning.

Alliums

Alliums (onions, leeks, chives, garlic, shallots, and scallions) oxidize the oxygen-transporting powerhouse hemoglobin. As a result, your dog can develop hemolytic anemia, a condition in which red blood cells die before the bone marrow has a chance to produce more.

SOURCES
Onion rings, dips, breadcrumbs; tomato sauce; sandwich meats; store-bought roasted chicken; dried spices; instant soup mixes; dietary supplements; et al.

 SAFETY TIPS
Check food labels carefully. Avoid giving your dog restaurant leftovers and prepared foods unless you know the ingredients.

 BEWARE
Any amount of allium consumption is unacceptable because it can cause damage on a cellular level where the effects of the damage are not noticeable.

Onions are more toxic than garlic.

 WHO KNEW?
Toxicosis typically occurs after consumption of a single large dose of onion or repeated small amounts of onion. Even ¼ cup can make a twenty-pound dog sick, while several cups may be needed to make a large dog sick.

Garlic contains only a tiny amount of the toxin that is bad for dogs, so many dog experts recommend small doses of garlic for overall health. Garlic is a natural antibiotic, it boosts the immune system, and it is a good flea preventative. It is also antifungal, antiviral, and antiseptic!

Caffeine

Caffeine is quite similar to the toxic chemical theobromine found in chocolate—it can damage the heart, lungs, kidney, and central nervous system.

Ingesting coffee can prompt seizures, abnormal heart rhythm, and death in dogs. Other caffeinated drinks—even tea—can have the same effect.

I asked for a decaf soy ten pump mocha latte with a caramel drizzle, not a skinny hazelnut macchiato with no whip!

SOURCES

 Coffee; tea; energy drinks and powders; diet pills; caffeine stimulants such as NoDoz; coffee-flavored treats such as ice cream; chocolate; et al.

SAFETY TIPS

Dogs will sniff out dis-carded coffee grounds in the trash and they seem to be attracted to them. Be careful when you discard coffee and keep things with caffeine safely out of reach.

BEWARE

 While a lick or two of most caffeinated beverages will not contain enough caffeine to cause poisoning in most dogs, the consumption of a moderate amount of coffee grounds, tea bags, or one or two diet pills could kill a small dog.

WHO KNEW?

Although the concentra-tion of theobromine in chocolate is three to ten times that of caffeine, both constituents contribute to the clinical syndrome seen in chocolate toxicosis.

Chocolate

Chocolate contains theobromine and caffeine, which are both toxic to dogs. Many dogs are attracted to the smell and taste of chocolate, making it a serious threat.

Are you eating chocolate? Is it milk or dark? Because the difference can mean a tummy ache or death.

chocolate

SOURCES

 Baker's chocolate; cocoa powder; chocolate pudding; chocolate ice cream; chocolate syrup; hot chocolate; cocoa mulch; white chocolate; baked goods such as brownies; candy; et al.

SAFETY TIPS

Don't put chocolate presents under the Christmas tree. Don't hide Easter candy where dogs can get at it. Don't leave Halloween candy (or any other candy) in reachable places.

What can I say, I'm dark, bitter, and bad for you—just one ounce of me can poison a 50-pound dog.

BEWARE

 Theobromine is more heavily concentrated in dark chocolate, making it more dangerous than milk chocolate. Unsweetened baker's chocolate contains eight to ten times the amount of theobromine as milk chocolate.

WHO KNEW?

 Mulch made out of cocoa? Yes, cocoa mulch consists of cocoa bean shells, and, like other chocolate products, contains theobromine and caffeine.

Grapes and Raisins

The root cause is currently unknown (some experts think that it may be due to a fungal toxin), but grapes and raisins are toxic to your pup. Dogs of any age, breed, or gender can be affected.

SOURCES

All types of grapes and raisins; currants; sultanas; grape juices and jams; fruit cake; cookies; trail mix; granola; et al.

SAFETY TIPS

It isn't understood why some dogs can eat grapes and raisins without harm, while others develop life-threatening problems. Some dogs who initially don't have an issue can develop one later on, so it is wise to avoid grapes and raisins entirely, particularly since there are so many safe alternatives such as apples.

BEWARE

Grapes and raisins can cause acute (sudden and severe) kidney failure, which can be deadly if not treated quickly.

WHO KNEW?

There is no safe dose of grapes or raisins. A dangerous/lethal amount may be as little as a few grapes or raisins. Even organic, pesticide-free grapes can result in toxicity.

Nuts

Many nuts can cause upset stomach, gastrointestinal obstruction, and poisoning. Packaged nuts may also contain salt and chemicals that can dehydrate or even poison dogs.

I'm no good for you . . .

ALMOND

BLACK WALNUT

ENGLISH WALNUT

HICKORY NUT

JAPANESE WALNUT

MACADAMIA

PECAN

PISTACHIO

SOURCES
Baked goods such as cookies, breads, cakes; trail mix; granola and granola bars; cereals; desserts; nut butters; et al.

BEWARE
Nutshells can tear tissue as well as create intestinal blockages.

Macadamia nuts are highly toxic to dogs, even in limited quantities. As few as six macadamia nuts can be toxic to a dog.

SAFETY TIPS
Check labels carefully.

Keep tempting nut treats (bowls of nuts, chocolate-covered nuts, nut-covered muffins and cakes) safely out of reach.

WHO KNEW?
According to Veterinary Pet Insurance, walnut poisoning is one of the most common claims for toxic ingestion.

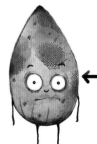

MOLDY NUTS ARE ESPECIALLY DANGEROUS.
Mold toxins can cause seizures, neurological distress, and liver problems.

Nutmeg

Nutmet's rich aroma can be very attractive to dogs. Unfortunately, nutmeg can damage a dog's central nervous system, cause tremors and seizures, increase heart rate and blood pressure, and if ingested in large enough quantities (and left untreated), nutmeg can be fatal. Exact quantities are unknown, but a good rule of thumb is that it would take a very large quantity to cause serious damage and death.

The small quantities often found in baked goods are highly unlikely to cause serious poisoning, but mild stomach upset can occur. Keep in mind that your dog's size and indivdual sensitivity to nutmeg can have a big impact.

I told her not to go up there.

Where's your sense of adventure?

SOURCES

Spice blends such as pumpkin pie spice; baked goods; French toast; eggnog; puddings; quiche; et al.

SAFETY TIPS

Never give your dog foods with nutmeg. Check labels carefully. Puppy-proof your spice drawer; dogs have been known to consume an entire bottle of nutmeg after chewing off the lid.

BEWARE

The small amount of nutmeg used in recipes is very unlikely to cause serious toxicity; however, if a very large amount is ingested your dog can suffer from tremors, seizures, nervous system issues, and even death.

WHO KNEW?

Nutmeg powder can be inadvertently inhaled, so it's wise to keep your dog away from the kitchen during food preparation.

Raw Salmon

"Salmon poisoning is a life-threatening condition most commonly caused by raw fish taken from coastal streams and rivers in the Pacific Northwest, from San Francisco all the way up to the coast of Alaska. Salmon, trout, lamprey, and other fish native to the Pacific Northwest can be carriers, as well as sculpin, redside shiner, shad, sturgeon, candlefish, and large-scale sucker."

—Dr. Karen Becker

Dogs are the only species susceptible to salmon poisoning.

SOURCES

Salmon (salmonid fish) and other anadromous fish (fish that swim upstream to breed) infected with the parasite *Nanophyetus salmincola*.

SAFETY TIPS

Do not allow dogs to eat raw fish. Thoroughly cook fish or freeze it for seven days first, which destroys the harmful parasites.

A key to diagnosis is telling your vet that your dog ate raw fish. If your dog raids trash cans, consider the possibility of SPD (Salmon Poisoning Disease).

BEWARE

Generally signs appear within six days of a dog eating an infected fish. If untreated, death usually occurs within fourteen days of eating the infected fish. Luckily, salmon poisoning is treatable if caught in time.

WHO KNEW?

"When a dog eats infected raw fish, the larval flukes release the rickettsiae organisms, which then travel in the bloodstream to the liver, lungs, brain, and lymphoid tissues, causing necrosis, hemorrhage, and hyperplasia."
—Dr. Karen Becker

I'm innocent!

Raw Yeast Dough

A twofold danger: Dough rises quickly after ingestion and can cause life-threatening stomach distention and obstruction. The fermentation of the yeast can lead to alcohol poisoning.

SOURCES

Yeast dough of any kind (bread, pizza, rolls); sourdough starter; et al.

SAFETY TIPS

Never leave raw dough where your dog can reach it, such as tables and counters—put it in the oven or cupboard while it's rising.

BEWARE

Fermenting yeast produces alcohol, which is rapidly absorbed into the bloodstream and can lead to alcohol poisoning.

WHO KNEW?

Most bread dough contains yeast. Your dog's stomach is the perfect warm, moist environment for yeast dough to expand rapidly and create a serious blockage.

The ASPCA's Animal Poison Control Center receives the majority of its raw bread dough poisoning calls during Christmas and Easter, so be extra vigilant during the holiday seasons.

Xylitol

Xylitol is widely used as a sugar substitute and filler. It is in a surprisingly wide array of foods, so check labels carefully because it can be deadly to dogs.

Many breath-freshening chewing gums, mints, oral rinses, and toothpastes contain xylitol, so I guess I'll just have to stop licking my butt and eating those tasty snacks the cat leaves for me in that box.

I'm not going to lie to you, Charles. Your breath smells like poop.

SOURCES
Chewing gum and mints; pudding and gelatin snacks; mouthwash and toothpaste; over-the-counter supplements (e.g., multivitamins, fish oils, etc.); low-calorie baked goods; cough syrups; chewable and gummy vitamins; peanut butters; et al.

BEWARE
Xylitol is extremely toxic to dogs. Small amounts of xylitol can cause life-threatening hypoglycemia (low blood sugar), liver failure, and even death.

Symptoms of xylitol toxicity develop rapidly, usually within fifteen to thirty minutes of consumption.

SAFETY TIPS
Make sure items containing xylitol are kept out of reach. Do not share any food with your dog that may contain xylitol. Only use pet toothpaste for pets, never human toothpaste.

WHO KNEW?
Xylitol is estimated to be one hundred times more toxic than chocolate.

MOSTLY NONTOXIC, BUT RISKY . . . PROCEED WITH CAUTION

Let's face it, most dogs love to eat and we often love to share our meals and snacks with them and spoil them with treats! Here are a few popular and common foods that we often give our dogs. Small amounts and certain types are OK, but they should never be fed in large quantities.

I'm just thinking that maybe if I only had one small bite it would be OK. . . .

Avocados

Avocados are loaded with healthy fats that are great for your dog's skin and coat. Avocados are are also loaded with an abundance of antioxidants that support the immune system. So why proceed with caution? Dogs often go after whole avocados and avocados contain a large pit in the center that—if ingested—can cause a serious blockage or obstruction in your dog's esophagus, stomach, or intestinal tract, so always exercise caution with whole avocados.

But it's so pretty.

Bones

There are benefits and risks to feeding your dog bones.

BENEFITS

Fun for dogs!

Mentally stimulating.

Good source of calcium, phosphorus, and trace minerals.

Good for dental health.

Exercises jaw.

RISKS

Can splinter— causing perforation and/or obstruction.

Choking hazard.

Can fracture and break teeth.

Sharp bone fragments can cause internal injuries if swallowed.

Bones contain a lot of calcium, which can be constipating.

Play It Safe with Bones

DO

Feed raw, fresh bones—preferably meaty ones. These take longer to chew, which is good for the teeth.

Feed frozen or partially frozen bones to slow a speedy-eater down.

Give large knuckle bones to dogs who tend to swallow things hole.

Monitor your dog closely and never leave him alone while he's chewing a bone.

DON'T

Feed cooked bones, which splinter more easily.

Give bones to dogs who've had dental work.

Feed too-small, cut-up, or sharp bones, which can cause injury and can splinter more easily.

Offer marrow bones, which are high in fat, frequently.

WARNING Cooked bones can be dangerous. They are more brittle than raw bones and splinter more easily. Raw bones, on the other hand, rarely splinter and are more easily digestible. The cooking process can also remove valuable nutrition.

 HANDY TIP If you're worried about giving your dog raw bones, give him a high-quality, edible dental bone to help control plaque and tartar, and to exercise the jaw muscle.

Dairy

Small amounts won't kill your dog, although you might be the recipient of some potent toots. Dogs are lactose intolerant and don't have enough of the lactase enzyme to properly digest dairy foods. If you are going to include dairy in your dog's diet, a good choice is kefir.

"These dairy or water-based grains have a multitude of vitamins and minerals. They provide a wide variety of probiotic organisms and have super awesome healing qualities."

—*Dogs Naturally* magazine

Fatty Foods

A dog's pancreas cannot sufficiently break down and process fatty foods. Too much fat in a dog's diet can lead to pancreatitis, as well as a host of other health issues.

WHO KNEW? Foods that are high in fat can cause vomiting and diarrhea. Pancreatitis often follows the ingestion of fatty meals in dogs. Certain breeds, including Miniature Schnauzers, Shetland Sheepdogs, and Yorkshire Terriers, appear to be more susceptible to pancreatitis than other breeds.

Fruit Pits and Seeds

Apple seeds, cherry pits, peach pits, and plum pits contain the poison cyanide. Additionally, pits and seeds can cause choking and bowel and intestinal obstruction.

I'm good! It's YOU guys who are bad.

Salt

Too much salt can lead to salt toxicity, which is extremely dangerous and potentially fatal.

BEWARE
There is no antidote for salt toxicity.

SALT IT MAKES EVERYTHING BETTER

 SOURCES
Homemade play dough; paint balls; water softeners; ocean water; roast drippings; jerky; potato chips; soup stock cubes; gravy powder; et al.

SAFETY TIPS
Dogs will happily drink ocean water, so make sure to take plenty of fresh water to the beach.

Avoid feeding all salty people food, such as jerky and potato chips, even if your dog gives you those eyes.

WHO KNEW?
Most homemade play dough recipes have high salt content. A toxic dose may be as little as one-sixteenth of a teaspoon per two pounds of body weight.

Sugar

This applies to food containing any and all sugars (high fructose corn syrup, brown sugar, maple syrup, honey, coconut sugar, etc.). Make sure you

check the ingredient label of human foods; seriously unhealthy high fructose corn syrup is found in just about every processed food. Too much sugar for your pup can lead to dental issues, obesity, and even diabetes.

Tomatoes

Tomatoes contain a substance called alpha-tomatine that can affect the heart adversely. Found throughout the entire plant, it is much more concentrated in the leaves and stem. Tomato plants also contain a toxic substance called solanine. Like tomatine, however, the amount of solanine found throughout the plant is extremely low, and a dog would have to ingest a massive amount to cause harm.

Green, unripened tomatoes contain more alpha-tomatine than ripe tomatoes.

The risk of death or serious illness from ingesting a tomato plant is low. If you feed your dog only a small amount of tomato, there should be no adverse effects (unless he is allergic). In fact, it is quite healthy because tomatoes contain a lot of beneficial vitamins.

> "Tomatine apparently binds to cholesterol in the digestive system, and the combination is naturally excreted, removing both tomatine and cholesterol. In fact this finding left them with the positive conclusion that tomatine may be beneficial in lowering undesirable levels of LDL cholesterol in animals."
>
> —Dr. Mendel Friedman of the Federal Department of Agriculture

Bonus!
Amazing Superfoods for Your Dog

Here are a few excellent foods that will provide a nutritional boost to your dog's diet, strengthening the immune system and improving overall health.

SU·PER·FOOD:
A nutrient-dense food considered to be especially beneficial for health and well-being.

This cake <u>definitely</u> qualifies as a superfood now.

Definitely.

Blueberries

These tiny fruits are packed with powerful antioxidants and vitamins. Studies have shown that dogs who eat blueberries have controlled blood sugar levels and may experience improved cardiovascular health. Blueberries can be beneficial to older dogs as studies have shown they may help with cognitive functions. Try fresh, frozen, and freeze-dried varieties.

Carrots

Loaded with phytonutrients and vitamins A, K, and C, carrots are a powerhouse of goodness. Carrots help a dog's vision, heart, and blood-sugar levels. Try fresh and cooked carrots, sliced and shaved.

Sweet Potatoes

Sweet potatoes contain more muscle-boosting amino acids than any of their cousins in the starch family. Research has shown that sweet potatoes help rid the liver of fatty cells and keep vital organs healthy. They are also a great source of fiber.

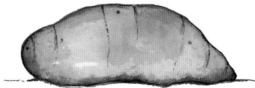

Flaxseed

Some health experts call it one of the most powerful plant foods on the planet.

Studies show that certain chemicals in flaxseed have antiangiogenic properties, which means the ability to stop tumors from forming new blood vessels.

Flaxseed promotes a healthy coat and skin with its omega-3 essential fatty acids. It also has been shown to have heart-healthy effects.

Flaxseed reduces inflammation.

Flaxseed contains alpha-linoleic acid, which offers benefits to the immune system.

Flaxseed is also an excellent source of fiber.

TIPS Flaxseed can go rancid quickly, so store it and flaxseed oil in the fridge in an airtight, preferably opaque container to keep them fresh and potent.

Whole flaxseeds are best if ground right before using.

Apples

These are wonderful fiber-filled treats for your dog. Apples are full of plant chemicals (phytonutrients) that are thought to be protective against some types of cancer in humans. They are a source of vitamins A and C and fiber. Apple seeds, however, contain cyanide, so your dog should not be allowed to eat the core. Though the effects of a few apple seeds will likely not harm your dog, the destructive effects can accumulate over time if you allow your dog to consume apple seeds regularly.

Fermented Foods

Fermented vegetables are bursting with probiotics (beneficial bacteria for gut health) and are alkalizing, which creates a hostile environment for cancer cells. They are also a very inexpensive way of turning good foods into superfoods: Try adding a little bit to your dog's meals every day. If you don't have time to make your own, many companies make excellent fermented foods.

FERMENTED FOODS ROCK!
- Keep bad gut bacteria in check.
- Loaded with natural enzymes.
- Inexpensive addition to any meal.
- Increase vitamin content.
- Improve digestion.
- Helpful for chronic conditions.

Spirulina

This microscopic algae houses a remarkable concentration of nutrients. It contains more protein than any other protein source ("Spirulina is 65 to 71 percent complete protein compared to beef, which is only 22 percent, and lentils, which are only 26 percent."—Dr. Mercola), plus cleansing chlorophyl, which helps the body get rid of toxins. It also has the highest concentrations of the rare and valuable essential fatty acid GLA (gamma-linolenic acid), as well as trace minerals, beta-carotene, and vitamin B-12. Studies confirm that spirulina helps strengthen the immune system, reduce the rate of cancer, and improve digestion. Spirulina is truly a superfood. In fact, NASA thinks it is a superior food and recommended that it be cultivated on long-term space missions.

SPIRULINA MAGIC "Scientists around the world—in Japan, China, India, Europe, Russia, and the USA—are discovering how and why spirulina is so effective for human and animal health. Hundreds of published scientific studies reveal how spirulina and its unique phytonutrients boost the immune system and improve health."

—*Dogs Naturally* magazine

Easy Sweet Potato Treat Recipe

Too many store-bought dog treats are loaded with unhealthy junk, so try this easy fiber- and vitamin-packed recipe!

preheat oven to 250°F.

1. **SCRUB**—but don't peel—one sweet potato. The skin is loaded with goodness!

2. **CUT** potato into slices (thinner for crispy, thicker for chewy).

3. **BAKE** for about three hours (really thin slices will bake much faster).

HIDDEN DANGERS

While most of us take great care to protect our dogs from obvious dangers such as ticks and speeding cars, here are some lesser known hazards to your dog's health and safety that you should know about.

Is it cookies?

Gastric Dilation and Volvulus (GDV)

This is a very serious and potentially fatal condition that needs quick action. Large-breed and deep-chested dogs seem to be more susceptible, but any dog is at risk, so knowing the signs and risk factors is crucial. Awareness can save your dog's life.

Signs of Deadly GDV

The stomach gets twisted at both ends, completely obstructing passages. This is very painful, causing your dog to pace or preventing him from wanting to move at all.

Attempting to vomit and belch, but cannot.

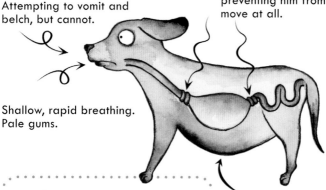

Shallow, rapid breathing. Pale gums.

SOME TIPS FOR PREVENTION

Feed smaller meals rather than one or two big meals per day to prevent eating too much, too fast (a lower rate of food consumption will help reduce the amount of air your dog swallows).

Discourage large amounts of water after meals.

Limit strenuous exercise before and after meals.

If your dog has a bloated stomach, is pacing, and is trying to vomit unsuccessfully, seek IMMEDIATE veterinary attention. If your regular vet is closed, go to a veterinary emergency center. Acting quickly is <u>key</u> to saving your dog's life.

"One of the most important things you can do to prevent a high-risk breed from developing GDV is to feed a species-appropriate diet containing no grains or other fermentable carbohydrates."

—Dr. Karen Becker, Mercola.com

Collar Asphyxiation

This is more common than you think; when dogs are playing, it is quite easy for one's jaw to get caught and twisted in another's collar. Dogs have choked to death and jaws have been broken because collars cannot be removed.

Common and potentially dangerous: A jaw can easily twist under a collar.

Quick Release or Breakaway Collars

One of these can be a wise investment for off-leash playtime. No collar that slips over the head should be used during playtime.

CRATES AND COLLARS

Consider removing any collar while crating your dog. If a collar gets stuck on the crate when no one is around, choking could be the result.

A brief word on crates: An open crate is a great retreat and "safe haven" for dogs that are fearful, but a closed crate should never be used for long periods of time. Leaving a dog in a crate all day while at work is cruel. Consider alternatives such as a room with access to fresh air, doggy daycare, or a willing neighbor or friend. For more information on the cruelty of crates, visit: peta.org/living/companion-animals/dog-crate-cage-prison.

Rat Bait

This is one of the most dangerous substances a dog can get into. It tastes and smells enticing. A dog can bleed internally within two hours of ingestion.

please don't kill me

RAT KILLER

Socks

Socks (as well as bras with gel inserts, undies, and pantyhose) can be enticing and are a major choking hazard. Vets frequently see dogs that have ingested a collection of undergarments.

Corn on the Cob

Although it is not toxic, the cob can cause intestinal obstruction—a very serious and potentially fatal condition (often requiring surgery for removal). Also, too many corn kernels can upset the digestive tract. Some dogs are allergic or sensitive to corn and can suffer intestinal issues as a result of eating corn.

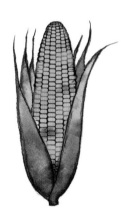

Allergies

Allergens can be inhaled, ingested, or come in contact with skin, making a dog's life pretty miserable if left untreated.

The most severe allergic reaction a dog can have is anaphylactic shock, which is life threatening and requires immediate action.

SIGNS OF ANAPHYLACTIC SHOCK: difficulty breathing/rapid breathing, swelling, diarrhea, vomiting, pale gums, trembling, fever, weakness. Pets can die of shock within ten to twenty minutes unless they get veterinary help immediately.

DOGS, LIKE PEOPLE, CAN BE ALLERGIC TO MANY THINGS:

- Foods
- Fleas and flea-control products
- Dust and molds
- Pollens
- Cleaning products
- Perfumes
- Rubber and plastics
- Fabrics
- Feathers
- And more

LEFT, MORE left, NO, RIGHT! Down, FASTER, UP, HARDER, no softer . . . ahhhhh

ALLERGIC REACTIONS INCLUDE:

- Itchy skin
- Itchy, runny eyes
- Vomiting and diarrhea
- Paw chewing/swollen paws
- Hair loss
- Scabby, red skin
- Ear infections
- Snoring

Allergies can develop at any time in your dog's life.

ALLERGY-BUSTING TIPS Strengthen your dog's immune system by avoiding unnecessary vaccinations and drugs. Try giving your dog "nature's Benadryl," quercetin, and omega-3 fatty acids—both reduce inflammation.

Dry Seaweed

Many dogs love to play with and eat dried seaweed found scattered on beaches at low tide and at the back of the beaches above the high-water mark. Seaweed, once ingested, absorbs moisture from the dog's digestive system and swells to incredibly large sizes in the gut. The result can be a blockage that prevents food from passing through the digestive system. If the problem isn't addressed quickly, the intestine could rupture.

Seaweed starts small . . .

. . . then greatly expands.

The bottom line—when walking on the beach, don't let your dog play with or eat seaweed.

Heatstroke

Dogs don't sweat like humans; their primary means of cooling down is panting. The number-one cause of fatal heatstroke in dogs comes from being left in a parked car. Keeping windows open or parking in the shade does very little to help keep a car's inside temperature cooler. It takes just minutes for a car's inside temperature to escalate, even on a cloudy, overcast day.

Some Signs of Heatstroke

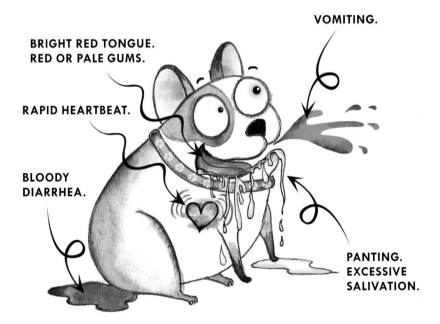

VOMITING.

**BRIGHT RED TONGUE.
RED OR PALE GUMS.**

RAPID HEARTBEAT.

**BLOODY
DIARRHEA.**

**PANTING.
EXCESSIVE
SALIVATION.**

Certain dogs are more susceptible to heatstroke. These include dogs with flat faces (e.g., Pugs, Bulldogs, et al.), thick coats, or heart or lung diseases, as well as black, elderly, or overweight dogs.

"On a hot day, a parked car can become a furnace in no time—
even with the windows open—which could lead to fatal heatstroke."

—Dr. Louise Murray, vice president
of the ASPCA Animal Hospital

Keeping windows
open won't make
a difference.

**EVEN IF IT IS ONLY 75°F OUTSIDE,
YOUR CAR CAN REACH AN INSIDE TEMPERATURE OF**
100°F IN JUST TEN MINUTES!

If you suspect your dog is suffering from heatstroke,
it is key to get him cooled down as quickly as possibly. Remove your dog
from the hot environment immediately. Place your dog in a tub, a shower,
or a baby pool, or use a hose (whatever you have access to) and coat
your dog with cool (not freezing cold) water—especially the head and
neck. Apply a cold pack or a bag of frozen veggies to your dog's head
to help lower body temperature. Vigorously rub/massage your dog,
which helps circulation and reduces the risk of shock. Let your dog drink
plenty of water, but don't force it. Seek immediate veterinary attention
after you stabilize your dog. Heatstroke can cause severe problems,
from brain swelling to kidney failure.

The best way to treat heatstroke is to prevent it.

KEEP COOL
Fans, ice cubes, frozen dog treats, kiddie pools, and sprinklers can all help keep your dog cool on hot days.

TRIM FUR
Trim longer fur, but never shave your dog—the layers of fur protect them from overheating and sunburn.

WATER

Always have fresh water available. Bring water with you on hikes and when you travel with your pup.

KEEP ME FILLED

LIMIT EXERCISE

Take walks early in the morning or late in the evening. Choose shady walks and avoid hot asphalt and sidewalks.

When temperatures are high, asphalt gets very hot. Dogs are close to the ground and can heat up quickly, and paws can burn.

HOLIDAY SAFETY

While we humans frolic and rejoice in food,
friends, and celebrations of the holiday seasons,
they can be a minefield of dangers for our dogs.
The holiday season is also the time of year that
pet poison hotlines receive the most calls.

Christmas Dangers

Snow Globes

Many snow globes contain toxic and deadly antifreeze, so keep them out of reach.

Chocolate on and under the Tree

Gift-wrapped chocolate under the tree and foil-covered chocolate tree ornaments pose a serious danger to dogs.

Your dog's sense of smell is more than 100,000 times greater than yours, so if you think they can't smell chocolate through giftwrap, think again.

Festive Foods

These are wonderful for us humans, but not always so good for our pups. Keep hazardous holiday treats safely out of your dog's reach.

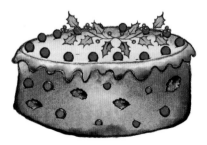

- Fruitcake often contains raisins, currants, and alcohol (all toxic)
- Chocolate (especially dark)
- Sweets and gum with deadly xylitol
- Raw yeast dough
- Fatty/salty meat scraps can lead to pancreatitis and salt poisoning

Choking Hazards

- Leftover wrapping paper
- Tree ornament hooks
- Toothpicks
- Wood skewers

TINSEL, ROAST STRING, AND RIBBON

These stringy things can wrap around the tongue or anchor in the stomach causing a blockage. Ingestion can cause a surgical emergency called a "linear foreign body" in the intestines. Tinsel can cut through intestinal tissue and cause severe damage.

MISTLETOE, HOLLY, AND THE CHRISTMAS TREE

Mistletoe and holly can be especially toxic to dogs. And Christmas trees are mildly toxic. Overall, it is a good idea to keep these holiday favorites safely out of reach of dogs who like to nibble.

POINSETTIA MYTH

This perennial holiday decoration is not the alarmingly dangerous plant that many people think, but it is mildly toxic, causing irritation in the mouth and stomach, and vomiting.

Easter Dangers

Plastic Easter grass can tangle around the tongue, the stomach, and bowels, which can result in serious internal damage requiring surgery.

Dogs love to chew on things, such as Easter baskets, many of which are treated with toxic chemicals, such as paint and gloss spray, which can cause stomach upset and even worse if swallowed. Select a safer alternative to protect your pooch.

Calls to pet poison helplines increase by 200 percent during the week of Easter because of chocolate.

Chocolate is toxic to dogs and sugar is just plain bad for dogs, so consider hiding Easter eggs in places your dog cannot reach.

Tell children about the dangers of chocolate for their dogs (see page 66).

Halloween Dangers

Glow Sticks and Glow Jewelry

The liquid inside these items does not cause systemic toxicity, but it is very bitter and can cause oral irritation.

Candy

Candy of any kind is not good for your dog, and chocolate, raisins, and many nuts are toxic.

Costume Caution

Small parts can be ingested.

Can freak dog out.

Can impair vision.

Can restrict breathing.

Can get very hot.

Fourth of July Dangers

BEFORE THE SPARKLY, FREAKIN'-LOUD FIREWORKS

I'm safe.
I'm loved.
Life is good.

THEN . . .

The sky is falling!
The sky is falling!

Fireworks

Not only are many dogs terrified of the loud sounds of fireworks, but they also can be severely burned. Many fireworks contain toxic substances such as heavy metals, potassium nitrate, and arsenic, so ingesting them can be a serious problem as well.

"July fifth is the busiest day of the year for animal shelters."

—American Humane Association

"[The day after the Fourth of July] shelters are inundated
with pets that panicked at the noise of firecrackers
and fled into the night, winding up lost, injured, or killed."

—Indiana Proactive Animal Welfare, Inc.

CALMING Consider giving your dog Rescue Remedy
(a homeopathic, natural way to help support calm
behavior in dogs during stressful situations) or relax-
ing herbs formulated for dogs, to take the edge off.

I.D. Identification tags are always important,
but they are crucial on the Fourth of July
when many pets go missing.

KEEP YOUR DOG INDOORS It may seem
obvious, but even if your pet is used to
being outside, the resulting panic caused
by fireworks or other loud noises may make
them break their restraint or jump a fence in
a terrified attempt to find safety.

Citronella

Items that contain citronella, such as candles, insect coils, and repellents,
are irritating toxins to dogs. Inhalation can cause severe respiratory
illnesses, such as pneumonia, and ingestion can harm your dog's
nervous system.

SAFETY FIRST

Being prepared can make a huge difference to the health and safety of your dog. Learning some basic skills, such as the Heimlich maneuver and rescue breathing (see page 113) and learning CPR (see page 127) could help save a dog's life one day.

Always keep these numbers visible and easily accessible. Every second counts in an emergency.

EMERGENCY CONTACT NUMBERS

- **YOUR VET**

- **24-HOUR VETERINARY EMERGENCY HOSPITAL**

- **POISON CONTROL HOTLINE**

It is also a good idea to keep medical records easily accessible.

DR. DOG

help?

Toxic Substances and Inducing Vomiting

If your dog gets into something poisonous, always call your vet or an animal poison helpline as soon as possible.

DO NOT INDUCE VOMITING

- If your dog is already throwing up.

- If your dog has lost consciousness, has a very low heart rate, is having difficulty breathing, is having convulsions/seizures, or is in shock.

- If your dog swallowed caustic substances such as bleach, drain cleaner, or battery acid.

- If your dog swallowed petroleum distillates such as gasoline or motor oil.

- If your dog has eaten something sharp or pointed.

- If it's been more than two hours from ingestion.

HOW TO INDUCE VOMITING

The general rule for hydrogen peroxide (only 3 percent) is one teaspoon per ten pounds of body weight, given orally. Repeat every fifteen to twenty minutes, up to three times, until the animal vomits.

3%
Hydrogen
Peroxide

Hiding the hydrogen peroxide in yogurt or ice cream (no chocolate!) may ensure that the hydrogen peroxide gets eaten.

First Aid Kit

It's a good idea to create a first aid kit for your home and to take with you when you travel. It is a good idea to keep your travel kit in a waterproof container.

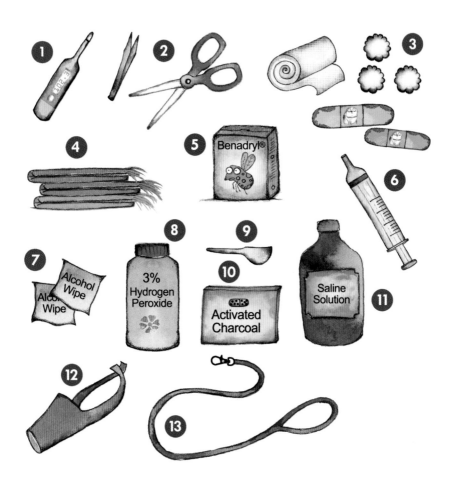

1. Rectal thermometer (and a lubricant such as petroleum jelly).

2. Tweezers and blunt-end scissors.

3. Gauze (can double as a muzzle to prevent stress biting, but never muzzle a dog who is coughing, having trouble breathing, or is nauseous); bandages; cotton balls.

4. Blankets and towels. Good for gently restraining and carrying a dog.

5. Diphenhydramine (Benadryl), if approved by a veterinarian, for bee stings and other allergic reactions. (The dosage is one milligram per pound of body weight.)

6. Syringe to flush eyes, clean wounds, or administer liquid medicine.

7. Alcohol wipes.

8. Hydrogen peroxide (only 3 percent) is a very versatile item. Use to induce vomiting (as directed by your vet) and clean wounds and ears. Hydrogen peroxide will flatten as it ages, so keep an unopened bottle handy.

9. Measuring spoon for dosing.

10. Activated charcoal or Milk of Magnesia. Give orally for ingestion of poisons. Consult with your vet or poison control before administering.

11. Saline solution to flush out eyes and clean wounds.

12. Muzzle for restraint for stress/fear biting.

13. Extra leash.

FIRST AID TIP
Dogs that are in pain, stressed, or scared may bite, so it is always good to muzzle a dog before attempting to administer first aid. Never muzzle a dog that is having trouble breathing, is coughing, or is nauseous.

Traveling with Your Dog?
Bring the Following Along

- Paperwork (storing in a waterproof bag is a good idea), including proof of rabies vaccination and important medical records.
- A current photo of your dog (in case he gets lost).
- Extra leash.
- Extra supply of your dog's medication.
- I.D. tag with vacation address (temporary tags are available).

Are we there? Are we there?
Need cookie. Need cookie now.
Pee-pee. Need pee-pee.
Maybe even a poo.

Heimlich Maneuver for Choking

Dogs that are choking will often panic. They may paw at the mouth in an attempt to remove the object. Another sign of choking is an unconscious dog. Dogs choke on everything from rubber balls to bones to sticks. Taking a few minutes to learn the Heimlich could save a dog's life one day. If you suspect choking, the first step is to always check the mouth for foreign objects.

1. Sweep finger(s) through mouth to dislodge or remove the object if you can. Pull tongue forward and use your fingers, tweezers, spoon handle, or needle-nose pliers to pry an object out of the mouth. Be careful not to push the object farther down the throat. If unsuccessful, try step two or three.

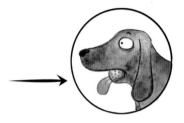

2. Pick up the dog's rear legs like a wheelbarrow and tilt him forward.

If tilting the dog does not work to dislodge the object, move on to perform the Heimlich maneuver.

3. MEDIUM/LARGE DOGS:

Stand behind dog.
Wrap arms around dog's belly.
Make a fist with hands.
Place fist on the soft
spot just below the rib
cage.

Thrust-pump UP and
FORWARD simultaneously,
in a quick/rapid manner.
Do five thrusts in quick succession.
Check for dislodged object
and remove it.

SMALL DOGS: Hug dog's back against your body.
Put fist (one-hand fist for very small dogs) on
the soft spot just bellow the rib cage. Thrust-pump
inward (toward your belly) and up (toward your
chin) simultaneously, in a quick/rapid manner.
Do five thrusts in quick succession. Check for
dislodged object and remove it.

If dog is lying down: Kneel right behind
dog's back. Make a fist with one or two
hands. Place fist on the soft spot just
below the rib cage.

Thrust-pump IN (toward you) and
UP (toward dog's head) simultaneously,
in a quick/rapid manner. Do five thrusts
in quick succession. Check for dislodged
object and remove it.

**AFTER five thrusts, check mouth for dislodged object and
remove it. If you don't see object, proceed to step four.**

4. If the Heimlich maneuver is NOT working after several attempts, try a series of quick thrusts with the palm of your hand between the dog's shoulder blades. Do this three or four times in a row.

If this does not work, try the Heimlich again, ideally while someone drives you to an animal hospital.

HEIMLICH MANEUVER TIPS

It is very important to remain calm. Animals can sense your panic.

After attempting the Heimlich with five thrusts, check mouth for object and try to remove it. Repeat.

Be careful when using this method because you can potentially damage a dog's internal organs if you apply too much force.

Be careful when handling a conscious dog under stress, as it may provoke them to nip or bite.

Get to an emergency vet as quickly as possible.

RESCUE BREATHING—If you <u>are</u> successful dislodging and removing the object, and your dog is <u>not</u> breathing:

SMALL DOGS With your mouth, cover and seal the entire snout (mouth and nose) and gently breathe into snout until chest rises.

LARGE DOGS Hold the muzzle closed. Place your mouth over the dog's nose and gently breathe into the nose until the chest rises.

Give four or five breaths quickly; check to see if dog is breathing without assistance. If breathing is shallow and irregular, continue giving dog rescue breaths for up to twenty minutes.

SMALL DOG Cover entire snout with your mouth.

LARGE DOG Hold muzzle closed and cover dog's nose with your mouth.

PREVENTION See your dog as the eternal toddler—always keep an eye on what your dog is chewing. Never leave him alone with chew sticks, bones, balls, toys, etc. Avoid toys and chew sticks that swell easily with moisture. Avoid toys with parts that can be easily chewed off and get stuck. Pick up enticing objects off the floor, from rubber bands to socks. Cut up large chunks of food, especially gristle.

BE VIGILANT AND PRESENT.

CHEWY

Bleeding

The most effective way to stop bleeding is to apply direct pressure to a wound.

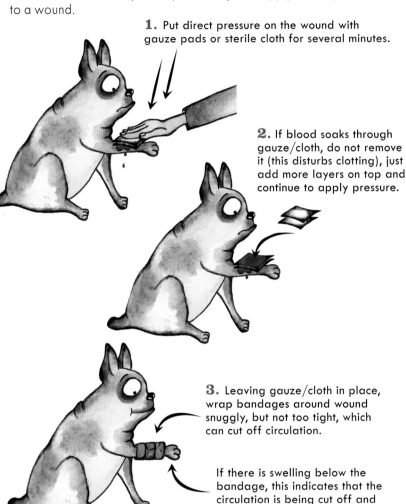

1. Put direct pressure on the wound with gauze pads or sterile cloth for several minutes.

2. If blood soaks through gauze/cloth, do not remove it (this disturbs clotting), just add more layers on top and continue to apply pressure.

3. Leaving gauze/cloth in place, wrap bandages around wound snuggly, but not too tight, which can cut off circulation.

If there is swelling below the bandage, this indicates that the circulation is being cut off and you need to loosen it.

Check frequently for swelling below bandage.

A tourniquet should ONLY be used as a last resort if you cannot stop the bleeding with direct pressure. A tourniquet can be used on the extremities and the tail.

Loop around leg and tighten. Always place tourniquet above the wound (between the wound and heart).

A tourniquet should be loosened every ten minutes to prevent tissue damage.

You can make a tourniquet out of gauze, a piece of cloth, rubber tubing, etc.

TIPS Before handling a wound, make sure your hands and materials are clean so wounds don't become infected.

If bleeding will not stop, continue to apply pressure or a tourniquet and get to your veterinarian as quickly as possible.

QUIZ

Yes-I'm-brilliant-and-remember-lots-of-bits-from-this-book quiz!

1. When you notice that your dog is not feeling well, what do you do?

A. Call your vet.
B. Take him shopping.
C. Ask him what he'd like for dinner.

ANSWER: A. Early detection and action can make a big difference for dogs, since they are often very good at masking pain. By the time you see it, a problem could be more developed than you think. So it is best to be on the safe side and call your vet.

2. Before performing the Heimlich maneuver, you should:

A. Wrap your dog in a blanket.
B. Check dog's mouth for foreign object.
C. Take dog's pulse.

ANSWER: B. Check dog's mouth for foreign objects because sometimes you may be able to dislodge the item causing the blockage.

3. What is a common food item that is toxic to dogs?

A. Apples
B. Shallots
C. Sweet potato

ANSWER: B. Shallots, which are part of the allium family, are toxic to dogs.

4. On a hot day, you can leave your dog in the car if:

A. The car is in the shade.
B. You leave all the windows open for good cross-ventilation.
C. Never leave your dog in the car.

ANSWER: C. Never leave your dog in the car even on a mild day. Car temperatures can escalate to dangerous heat very quickly even on a 70°F cloudy day.

5. What is a sign that your dog is not feeling well and needs veterinarian attention?

A. Pale or bluish gums.
B. Licking your face nonstop.
C. Fur shedding all over sofa.

ANSWER: A. Pale or bluish gums. Call your vet; a dog's normal gum color is a healthy pink.

6. Periodontal disease is serious and can lead to secondary diseases such as heart disease. What is the best thing you can do to help avoid this?

A. Play ball with a tennis ball.
B. Brush your dog's teeth regularly.
C. Rub your dog's gums with your fingers.

ANSWER: B. Brushing your dog's teeth regularly will help keep your dog healthy and happy. And playing ball with a tennis ball is not a great idea because the fuzzy fibers can wear your dog's teeth down over time.

7. What should you do if your dog is stung by a bee?

A. Pull the stinger out.
B. Leave your dog alone and he will work it out.
C. Scrape the stinger out with a credit card or other firm edge.

ANSWER: C. Scrape the stinger out with a credit card or other firm edge. Using your fingers or tweezers may force more venom out of the stinger and into your dog. Apply a compress of baking soda and water to sooth the area, and watch your dog for signs of a severe allergic reaction. Your vet may advise you to administer Benadryl to relieve symptoms.

8. During the Fourth of July you should make sure that your dog is:

A. Wearing identification.
B. Wearing a patriotic item of clothing.
C. Close to the fireworks, so he can see the pretty sparkles.

ANSWER: A. Wearing identification. July fifth is the busiest day of the year at animal shelters because pets bolt. If your dog is wearing an I.D., it will help him get back home safely. Even better, make sure your dog is safely inside and not outside during the festivities.

9. If your dog has been bitten by a snake you should:

A. Suck the venom out of the bite wound.
B. Keep him calm and take him to the vet immediately.
C. Wrap your dog in a blanket and cover the wound with gauze.

ANSWER: B. Keep him calm and take him to the vet immediately. If you can, you should also take a photo of the snake for proper identification. Keep in mind many snakes are not venomous and there are such things as a "dry" bite with no venom being released. But always be cautious and go to the vet for immediate help.

10. What can be deadly to your dog?

A. Xylitol.
B. Gelatin.
C. Spirulina.

ANSWER: A. Xylitol. This is extremely toxic to dogs. Small amounts of xylitol can cause life-threatening hypoglycemia (low blood sugar), liver failure, and even death. Symptoms of xylitol toxicity develop rapidly, usually within fifteen to thirty minutes of consumption.

If you love me, you'll get all the answers right!

A BRIEF WORD ON ADOPTION

I'm always amazed at how many people buy a dog when shelters are overflowing. But then I remind myself that many people simply don't know that shelters are brimming with adorable dogs, and more importantly people don't know that shelters are brimming with dogs that are not only adorable but also perfectly <u>normal</u> and <u>healthy</u>.

Every year millions of dogs and cats are killed in shelters.

What many people also don't realize is that now more than ever, with the help of online services such as Adopt-a-Pet.com, you can find exactly what you're looking for: tiny white dog; big slobbery pup; German Shepherd; Golden Retriever. Chances are these pups and more are waiting patiently for you right now at your local shelter or rescue.

Dear Lord, can you please find homes for all the shelter dogs like my beloved Skippy? Amen.

Common Myths about Shelter Dogs

1. Shelter dogs are damaged goods: False!
The vast majority of dogs in shelters are wonderful family pets who have been given up by their owners. Many families give up their dog because of the following:

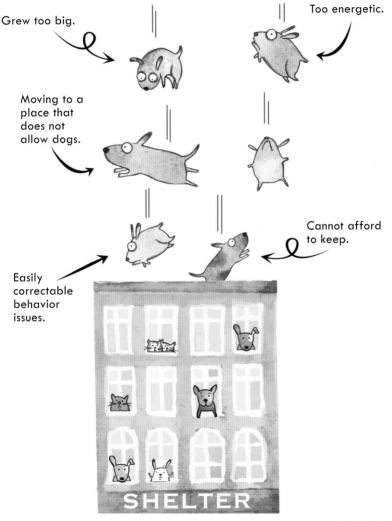

Grew too big.

Too energetic.

Moving to a place that does not allow dogs.

Cannot afford to keep.

Easily correctable behavior issues.

SHELTER

Behavior issues are rarely the reason dogs end up in shelters. And if it is the reason, then a little love, training, and patience can easily correct the problem. Dogs want nothing more than to please their humans and training them gives them that opportunity.

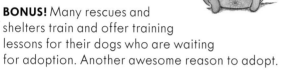

BONUS! Many rescues and shelters train and offer training lessons for their dogs who are waiting for adoption. Another awesome reason to adopt.

2. **You don't know what you're getting with a shelter pet: False!**
Veterinarians, vet techs, and animal specialists volunteer at shelters, so they often know a dog's personality and temperament. In addition, many shelters/rescues offer home visits and fostering programs so you can give the dog a test run. Most shelters have visiting rooms, where you can get to know a dog better before committing. Many dogs up for adoption are in foster care, so you'll know if the dog is good with other dogs, cats, and children. You'll also learn other valuable information about a dog.

3. **Shelters won't have exactly what I'm looking for: False!**
With online sites such as Adopt-a-Pet.com, you can find exactly what you are looking for. And if they don't have a particular dog immediately available, you can sign up to be alerted when dogs matching your criteria come into the system.

According to studies, more than 25 percent of pets in shelters are purebred dogs and cats. Breed rescues are widespread—offering everything from toy breeds to Golden Retrievers to Pit Bulls.

4. Adoption fees are too expensive: False!

Most rescue and shelter dogs come with lots of necessary items and services already paid for such as spay/neuter operations, rabies and other vaccinations, flea preventative, and heartworm and Lyme disease tests. All of these can easily add up to hundreds and hundreds of dollars. You won't find a breeder's dog or a store-bought pup that comes with all of these things taken care of for you.

Shelter and rescue dogs come with many necessary things prepaid.

Store-bought and breeder dogs do not.

Also, knowing that you're saving a life is a pretty priceless bonus, wouldn't you say?

Do something amazing today and consider giving a homeless dog a wonderful, warm home.

TIP Consider adopting an adult dog. They come with many bonuses—you'll know their full size and much of their temperament, and many will be house-trained as well. If you prefer watching movies to running marathons, then consider adopting a senior dog who would love nothing more than a few last years of happiness and love.

RESOURCES
Pet Poison Hotlines

ASPCA ANIMAL POISON CONTROL

The ASPCA's specially trained staff of veterinary toxicologists have access to an extensive database and are able to diagnose problems and give treatment advice quickly. The ASPCA has experience with more than two million cases involving drugs, pesticides, plants, metals, and other potentially hazardous items.

PHONE 1-888-426-4435

HOURS 24 hours a day, 365 days a year

PET POISON HELPLINE

Pet Poison Helpline is a 24-hour animal poison control service available throughout the United States, Canada, and the Caribbean. They have board-certified veterinary specialists: internal medicine (DACVIM), emergency critical care (DACVECC), and veterinary toxicologists.

PHONE 1-800-213-6680

If you're calling from Puerto Rico or the U.S. Virgin Islands, you can reach Pet Poison Helpline toll-free at 877-416-7319. Other Caribbean islands can reach them at 011-1-952-853-1716.

HOURS 24 hours a day, 7 days a week

Online Pet Adoption Resources

ADOPT-A-PET.COM North America's largest nonprofit pet adoption web service. Easily search hundreds of thousands of adoptable pets by breed, size, location, and more.

PETFINDER.COM Home of hundreds of thousands of adoptable pets.

Spay/Neuter Resources

ASPCA.org has a comprehensive and searchable database designed to help people find low-cost spay/neuter programs in their community. Visit www.aspca.org/pet-care/spayneuter.

Dog/Pet First Aid Books

Dog First Aid, by the American Red Cross

The First Aid Companion for Dogs & Cats, by Amy D. Shojai

The Safe Dog Handbook, by Melanie Monteiro

Pet First Aid App

The America Red Cross has the free app "Pet First Aid by American Red Cross."

CPR and First Aid Classes

Local veterinarians and animal hospitals may offer classes. There are online courses at Pet Tech (PetTech.net). You can also check with the American Red Cross.

ACKNOWLEDGMENTS

To every single one of you magnificent readers: The fact that you're holding this book in your hands says you care about protecting your pups, and that is worth a vigorous and heartfelt thank-you!

I'm grateful to the many friends and family members who took time out from their busy lives to help me with this book. A big thanks to my sister-in-law, Kathryn Donnelly Luwis, for her astute proofreading and her contagious enthusiasm. Thank you to my "big sister" Billie Tooley, whose encouragement always carries me through the dark spots. Thanks to my incredible brothers, Tim and Brian, for always believing in me. An over-sized thank-you to my mama, Brenda Jean Luwis, who marvels at all my creations, which is more precious to me than words can convey. I love you to the moon and back!

I'm immensely grateful to my agent, Myrsini Stephanides, who works quietly behind the scenes on my behalf, and to my lovely and clever editor, Patty Rice—I'm lucky that you both love my work and make me feel like a million bucks when I sometimes feel like half a penny.

To my special friend Terry Thiel, who deserves an acknowledgment page all to herself because she generously shares her clever and dazzling brain with me: You are my confidante and partner in all crime.

To two amazing animal champions and dear friends, Jannette Patterson and Ingrid Newkirk: Thank you for constantly working on behalf of animals, and for inspiring me to live a cruelty-free life and to always speak up where there is animal abuse.

Drawing and writing involves hours of solitary work, so I thank my precious, darling dog, Isabelle, for keeping me company, and for keeping my feet warm through the often challenging and lonely process of creating a book.

Last, but most of all, to my heart-crushingly adorable and brilliant husband, Bryan Aspey, who is my indispensable second pair of eyes in all things creative: I will love you forever.

ABOUT THE AUTHOR

Amy Luwis is an animal lover and animal advocate, and cofounder of the nonprofit Adopt-a-Pet.com— North America's largest nonprofit pet adoption website. Amy is passionate about ending animal abuse and educating the public about being compassionate toward all creatures great and small.

Amy lives and works in Los Angeles, California, with her husband, musician/composer Bryan Aspey, and their adopted pit bull, Isabelle, as well as a rotating menagerie of foster dogs.

Have a dog safety story? Amy would love to hear from you!

Follow Amy!
RedandHowling.com
facebook.com/RedandHowling
Instagram: @RedandHowling

Then what?

INDEX

Andrews McMeel Publishing
a division of Andrews McMeel Universal
1130 Walnut Street, Kansas City, Missouri 64106

www.andrewsmcmeel.com

16 17 18 19 20 SDB 10 9 8 7 6 5 4 3 2 1

ISBN: 978-1-4494-7230-6

Library of Congress Control Number: 2015957532

Editor: Patty Rice
Art Director: Julie Barnes
Production Manager: Tamara Haus
Production Editor: Erika Kuster

All plant photos: public domain

KG Flavors and Frames font by Kimberly Geswein Fonts

ATTENTION: SCHOOLS AND BUSINESSES
Andrews McMeel books are available at quantity discounts with bulk purchase for educational, business, or sales promotional use. For information, please e-mail the Andrews McMeel Publishing Special Sales Department: specialsales@amuniversal.com.

Put a copy in the bathroom and you know they'll read it for sure.

I love this book.